The flow...

By Jenny Giles
Illustrated by Liz Alger

Mom and Dad
and James and Nick
are at a wedding.

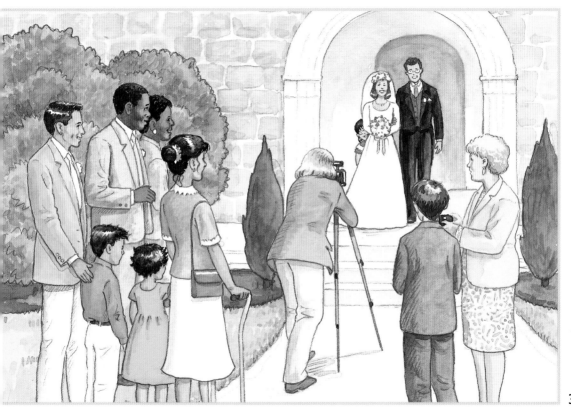

Kate is at the wedding, too.
Kate is the flower girl.

"Look, Nick,"
said Mom.
"Can you see Kate?
Kate is in the photo.
Look at Kate's flowers."

"Look at
the wedding cars,"
said James.
"Come and see
the cars, Dad."

"Flowers!" said Nick.
"Flowers for me."

"Oh, no!
Look at Nick!"
said Dad.

"**Nicola!** Come here!"

"Oh, no!" said Mom.

James said,
"Nick is in the photo!"

"Look at me," said Nick.

"I am a flower girl, too."